salmonpoetry

*Celebrating 35 Years
of Literary Publishing*

Only More So

Millicent Borges Accardi

Published in 2016 by
Salmon Poetry
Cliffs of Moher, County Clare, Ireland
Website: www.salmonpoetry.com
Email: info@salmonpoetry.com

ISBN 978-1-910669-28-0

COVER IMAGE: © *Mistertwister* | *Dreamstime.com*
COVER DESIGN & TYPESETTING: *Siobhán Hutson*
Printed in Ireland by Sprint Print

To Charles

Acknowledgments

Grateful acknowledgment is extended to the following publications in which these poems (or earlier versions) first appeared:

Blue Mesa Review:"For Lynda Hull"
Chariton Review: "Whatever"
Hubbub: "Somewhere in Prague," "The Well"
Interim: "Raising Butterflies"
International Poetry Review: Hispanic Edition: "Swinging Open"
Luna Luna: "Mother Ditch"
Madison Review: "Only More So"
Mid-American Poetry Review: "The Well."
New Delta Review: "Like Nameless Skyscrapers."
New Letters: "Coupling"
Nimrod: "Ordinary Fears," "Leading, me Towards Desperation," "Inventing the Present"
Rio: A Journal of the Arts: "Ordinary Fears," "A Question of Desire"
Southern California Anthology: "The Misses"
Sulphur River Literary Review: "Faith."
Sycamore Review: "Renovation"
Timber Creek Review: "Coupling"
Tampa Review: "In Prague," "This is What People Do"
Wallace Stevens Journal: "On a Theme by William Stafford"
Westerly Centre for Literature, Australia: "Ethnic Cleansing," "Portrait of a Young Girl 1942."
Witness: "Buying Sleep"

Special thanks to the National Endowment for the Arts, the California Arts Council; CantoMundo; FLAD (Luso-American Foundation in Portugal); the Corporation of Yaddo; Jentel; Fundación Valparaíso in Mojacar, Spain; and Barbara Deming Foundation (Money for Women) for their generous support and encouragement.

A few poems from this book are included in the anthologies: *Gavea-Brown Book of Portuguese American Poetry and Writers of the Portuguese Diaspora in the United States and Canada: An Anthology* as well as in the chapbook entitled *Woman on a Shaky Bridge*.

Contents

On a Theme by William Stafford   11

Coupling   12

Ciscenje Prostora   13

Only More So   15

Buying Sleep   17

The Misses   18

Portrait of a Girl, 1942   19

If World War Two Had Ended in Germany
the Same Over-night Way that Socialism Did   20

The Night of Broken Glass   22

In Prague   23

How to Shake off the Políciade Segurança Pública Circa 1970   24

This is What People Do   26

Widow   28

In a Certain Village   30

Summer Vacations   32

For Lynda Hull   34

Breaking with the Old   35

If I Had Not Read the Book, I'd Still Have Believed   36

Musings in January   37

Arriving at the Place of the Pain   38

Sundown Town   39

Start Here   40

Renovation   41

Arrhythmia 42

The Well 43

Like Nameless Skyscrapers 45

Swinging Open 47

Together with me, Remember 48

Under Different Conditions 49

The World in 2001 51

Amazing Grace 52

Whatever 53

The Story of the Stories 54

Watering Day 56

Almonds 57

Portuguese Bend 58

Mother Ditch 60

After She Got her Nose Fixed 62

There Was a Part 63

The Last Borges 65

Inventing the Present 67

Ordinary 68

What the Water Gives Me 69

The Mass 70

Honest Words 72

Faith 74

On a Theme by William Stafford

If I could be like Wallace Stevens,
I'd fold my clothes into the bureau
drawer instead of living
from a suitcase. I'd hang up my long
coat in the closet and really move
in.

I'd cook food in my room on a hot
plate, then open up the window for
the neighbors. With my tongue
pursed like a stick, I'd push my ice
cream all the way down to the end,
so that even the last bite contained
both cone and cream.

Coupling

The woman thought she would be good,
making sure he washed,

rescuing black stockings, wood pile
scraps. Finding theatre tickets

and collecting parking stubs.
She thought she would be good

at using his soap. Remembering
not to wear perfume and waking

up to call home. In the hotel,
hiding while the hot water ran,

her heart compact as plywood.
She thought she would be good

at belonging. The bulk of her time
a two-by -four dove-tailed into a corner,

getting the best he had to offer.
She thought she had a talent for being aloof.

On him, she made few demands.
When he was away, she imagined

his heart open, fearless
hands holding a piece of wood steady

while a diamond-point blade cut through.

Ciscenje Prostora

(Ethnic Cleansing)

This woman does not know he
carries the devil's four poster bed
in his palm, clutching it like promised
money: Bosnia, Croatia, Serbia, home.

She can't predict the hour
he will climb the steps, laughter
echoing behind him, his boots
scraping the stone, his steps
following her mother's call.

She only knows that the rebel tanks,
with nudies plastered to their sides,
are rolling through her town, shaking houses
like wind, carving up the patterns of the land.

She knows not to stare back
when he finds her, hiding behind a clay
pot. When his soldier's eyes become her
life, more understandable than her or me or any
pronoun she whispers out between no and help,
she shuts her eyes, imagining cold weather.

He tries the rug of her family's house
with the slant of his hips, dragging
her shoulders along behind him.

Her skin beneath his, now
this skin that he uses for the rhythm
of bodies, now pushed up against
a wall, this skin he now needs, this drumming beat,
this having nothing to lose.

Serbia, Bosnia, Croatia; the countries undulate
together while he dances the dance of the basilisk
thighs marching, marching.

Even little sounds, like birds overhead,
encourage him to go on, to spit, to breathe
three generations of her surrender into his lungs.

Then, silence.
Lost territories, rebels, food, clothing, shelter,
she thinks not of peace, but of surviving
the winter, of outlasting the enemy, of winning.

Only More So

You see it was very much like this.
In the flatland dregs, the fat-coated
soldiers knocked at the door, so a woman
was forced, with a gritty smile,
to invite them in, to sit by her
yellow fire, to swallow up her walls.

In the corner her husband rubbed
a wooden rifle, tapped wooden boots against
a wooden floor, thinking, thinking
visitors are cold as bad luck.
He looped his fingers under his belt
and turned to gravel.

The soldiers, making circles in the dust
on the hearth, asked the woman to remember
the unremembered: the jewelry sold for food,
the Moravian lace curtains.

Where are the rings? Two and now one?
The woman spun her wedding band around her
finger and gave them her best,
"we were here before you" silver glare.

Surrounded by dust and half-opened words,
the woman's mottled eyes brought a dull patina
to the repeated questions. The sharp wool collars
of the soldiers pointed south; inside,
the crudely made benches evaporated into firewood.

It was like this: the woman's hips swayed
like harmonicas when the men watched her fetch
water and run it into the basin, cracking
ice with her fingernails.

They asked her, Why do trees mean? and
What does water stand for?
while their stares mocked the broken
windows, and pain, itself, counted the woman's
buttons as they easily slipped through the stitching
of her clothes.

You see it was all so simple:
they wanted the smooth golden of her neck,
the warm nest of her skirt;
her loss shifting like daggers beneath their skin.

As wind fragmented, as doors burned,
as fires latched, the last woman, this last
woman, clasped a bowl to her chest knowing, knowing,
what the snow outside pretended, knowing
that nothing important ever belonged to her.

That now she must survive by owning air,
holding back the red, the full, the bare,
the proud canvases of flat language paper
that once told her everything she needed
to know.

It was like this, only more so.

Buying Sleep

My brother leans over
in the cabin bedroom
that we shared once
a year and says to me
—now mind you
this is the brother I have
hated all my life—
he leans over the bunk bed.
Yes, he got the top.
He leans
into the springs
like he's an old car
all 12 years
of him, and he
says to a boy half his age,
a boy tossing and fearing
outhouse snakes,
and the awful windy
silence, the calm of the desert
and the unfed
spring of the fear of Father
for still being awake
when the rest
of the sane world is not.
Now this brother leans over
and asks in the sweetest voice possible:
"Wanna buy some sleep?" In the darkness
I nod and, then, realizing years later
say, "Yes," aloud and so he begins.
He gathers up a cocoon of sleep
in his hands and tucks in my feet,
my ankles, my legs, my torso
and then zips it up tightly under my chin
almost as if he loved me.

The Misses

I'd like to think that she misses
him. Although, I'm not sure
if she does, but I imagine
her missing him in the curves
of her mouth, in the way she tosses
her hands likely in the air, letting them
fall around her like thin parachute silk,
and then pausing for a moment.

It's not apparent in her voice
but the tone has changed, deepened,
somehow, lengthened like growing
stalks of wheat before harvest,
every moment in danger of being
blown over, of being bent against
even the breeze, yet loftier than
they have ever been before.

The true misses in our lives are so rare
that they are larger than us, though
also more fragile than the entire world.

I imagine her walking to Norm's Knob
in Indiana breathing heavy with smoker's lungs,
struggling up the narrow low inclined hill,
looking for him in the setting sun,

watching the power of the orange,
the yellow, the white, shutting
her eyes from the weight
of brightness, the last flash
as the sun and memory both disappear,
meeting soil at the point of no return,
the highest point of their lives.

Portrait of a Girl, 1942

Based on the Jan Lukas photograph of Vendulka Vogelova, taken a few
hours before the young girl was transported to a concentration camp.

I am the mirror for one who speaks;
these fresh gaps are wind in the linden trees,
cotton flowers of life. A mirror is not much
for all of us, but if we listen for reflection,

the clear twin face of a groan behind the looking
glass, we hear the cat's hair sounds of all people
grumbling in the same manner about the air
the food the earth the sidewalk.

I am the mirror for all the world's silence,
and the ones who slipped through without drawing
blood, whose suicides number nothing next
to vast doors too tall to reach heaven, locked
forever, whose breaking takes generations,
sometimes, dull copper paint on the back of a lake.

I am the mirror for one who is trembling
like a child who has noticed too much, eyes
hard olive pits. I think about how life
cracks when the vanity glass overturns
our hands. Sharp pints in bars. Uneven edges
of ale. Crisp indignities of foam.

I am the mirror for all who choose
not to speak. I crack
in the dark. I shine in the snow.

If World War Two Had Ended in Germany the Same Over-night Way that Socialism Did

The next day, the remaining
Yellow stars would have fallen
To the motherland. The swastikas
Would be recalled. The gas
Chambers, they might grind
To a seeking, brilliant halt.
Slowly, but, at first there would
Be a few more rounds
Of backed up holocaust traffic,
The thirteenth loaf of a baker's
Dozen you might say. All the Jews
Would come out of hiding, calling,
"I'm no longer
'It'" and "Olly Olly oxen free."
Those who had emigrated
Would return on gilded wings, dipping
Into baskets of keys to houses in
Names of cities no longer there.
The nazis would have forgotten
The goose step over-night,
And all dress parades in Berlin
Would be immediately canceled
Due to rain. The SS's false politeness
Perhaps replaced by sour words,
And the anti-Semite puppet show in
Adolph square would continue
Only for another
Week, Punch and Judy preempted.
Those in the hills would not hear
The news until months later.
The transports to the labor camps
Would run
Out of petrol and sprout flat tires.
The human scalp lampshades and hair

Sweaters unsold. The bottom
Would drop out of the market
For melted gold teeth. The dark
Green numbers tattooed on arms
Would all be surgically removed.
And the children's toys, the wooden
Tops and doll houses left during better times,
Would all find new owners. The relatives
On the block would return as if they had been
Away at finishing school. Anne Frank and Peter
Would get married and live happily ever after.
The leftover bones would be piled up and burned
Like ordinary rubbish. Knitted caps of kitten's
Fur, Hitler youth model bicycles and books
Containing Aryan history lessons would go out
Of fashion. The temples would be joyfully reopened,
The synagogues would have housewarming parties.
The *Kushrüt* signs would be nailed
To delicatessen storefronts, and rabbis
Would be handed their *tzitzit* and reinstated
To neighborhood posts. The glass would be broken
Under the groom's heel at weddings again;
And canters would sing. *Masel tov* would be heard
On corners. It would be just like when prohibition
Was repealed or the abolishment of slavery.
A freedom would be returned, a freedom, that had been
Previously lost. After Hitler, all countrymen would be
Left standing, legs apart, ready to greet the returning Jews.

The Night of Broken Glass

The essential business of living well
Continued on in the shops and towns
And villages even as windows were
Smashed and glass covered the streets
In pieces of shrapnel that reflected
The stars in the night sky like rays
Of yellow sunshine.

The essential business of living well
Were days covered in pieces,
A quarter of civilization, ninety one
Men ransacked like windows
With sledgehammers and hatred.

In Vienna alone, 95 prayers
Were set on fire, a long history
Of normalcy, bent on blackening
Out the news before the rest
Of the world could undo the nasty
Fairytale hint of a brief story that
A group of people did not want told.

The essential business of living well
Continues in shock waves
That falls into the ground of innocent
People, triggered inside a soul
Of nothingness that pretended
To solve an impossible equation.

In Prague

Men jackhammer the corner of Jilska and Mickalska,
disturbing the air's intonation. The exposed
sewer pipes, inches from open graves, lie like illness.
As we watch, morning beaten from bodies escapes
in a white whirl of cameos, sand, and milk.

Here, Rodina means nothing.

A skull, embedded in a dirt wall seems, for a moment,
as white and round as bread. Jaws, on metal stands,
tagged with numbers, wait for a turn to be whole again.

Here, dates are rounded to the nearest hundred.

Tarsals, femurs, ulna, open-pored
bones like coral, spinal cord beads
on strings, legs bowed, dried marrow
dark as tunnels, joints like fists, teeth.

Here, there are no pebbles of prayer left behind.
All is traffic, swollen construction, boroughs
and picture taking, stripping the city's bark
blind with concrete.

Not what I want. So, leave this place
and take me where bones don't mean treasure, where the
air is heavy, where graves
are planted like corn rows, and evening settles like water.

Take me where stones are full
enough for stones and death is a long rope
wrapped around kin I cannot have,
wisdom for the hungry, thumb-prints

for the innocent, tombs for generations.
Take me where memory makes my legs move.
Take me where moss holds language.
Take me where we have a name for the things we do.

How to Shake off the Polícia de Segurança Pública Circa 1970

Walk home
determined, neither
urgent nor pokey.
Make clear cut
turns and hold
your head up high.
Carry an ordinary
briefcase. Dress
in shades of brown,
as if you could fold
up and turn back
into dirt if you
needed to. Do not
stop or pause except
to honor street lights
and stop signs. Stay
in the shadows,
but do not hug them
or stay tight
to the overhangs.
Do not pause
To peer into windows,
or look as if you are
waiting for someone
like Salazar.
Disappear. Disappear.
Disappear, as best you can
into traffic
or the pulse of Lisboa.
Do not hesitate
When the men draw
closer, turn into the nearest
side street, that is dimly lighted.
Find a building

where people are entering
easily. Go up the stairs
as if you have business
there, or as if this is your
own home, which it isn't.
Do not look back even
cautiously at the PSP,
glance down, step with surety
into the unfamiliar lobby.
Find the stairs. Sit
in the darkness under
until you have
become the earth. Hold
your breath
until the men have gone
by. Tell yourself you are safe
and everything
is fine. Remain curled up
longer than you have to,
longer than you imagine might
be necessary before
you regroup and head back.

This is What People Do

They move to Mukilteo and throw
pots or play on the senior soccer league.
They set up a weight room and deliver cellular
phones. They get proverbially married and
have hope for children, saying this generation
will be different. They watch Little House on
the Prairie and cry when Mary goes blind.
They get laid off from the oil company
and go back to art school. They have five
or six kids and wait while their wife has
schizophrenic episodes where she thinks
the oldest child is God. They retire to places
called Happy Acres and Leisure World.
They get hired by the Honolulu Fire Department
and moonlight as a Congressman. They buy
a house with a pool on Mount Washington,
then get a divorce. They have a brother with
pancreatic cancer. They recycle the garbage for
the entire building. They visit ground zero in
New York. They buy a $10,000 Italian
bed and furnish the flat in Sinatra's orange.
They let their wife work in a bank and stay
home playing Scrabble and pretending to
write grants for Planned Parenthood. They
drive through snow storms in Palmdale
and install plants at the MGM in Las Vegas.
They live down the hall and do not answer
their phone. They are married for 18 years,
then take up with an old high school sweetheart
they found on the internet who stalks them.
They get restraining orders. They bail their
Japanese friends out of jail for DUIs and hear
about how they were tossed around in the cell.
They go to Little Tokyo and sleep in their car.
They rent a love nest in downtown Los Angeles
and walk to work. They go to the Queen Mary

once a month and run the ham radio room.
They turn 80 and have a surprise party thrown
for them at the Airport Marriott. They adopt
three cats and name them TS Eliot, Sylvia Plath
and Bartleby the Scrivener. They go to London
for New Year's. They do not answer the phone
unless it rings twice, times eight. Their mailbox
is not emptied. They wait until the last
minute and show up at the Hollywood Bowl,
getting box seats for Tony Bennett, then go back
stage and meet Pete Samprass. They like
salami sandwiches, dry. They drink Korbel
and smoke Nat Sherman's. They wish they lived
in New York City and did not have to drive.
They get belligerent in a pub called Dead Poets.
They wait in line for jazz at Smoke. They like Miles
Davis and not just because an ex-husband did.
They travel or they don't. Everyone is always so happy
when they are finally alone. They do the Friday dance
in the kitchen while Sublime plays on the Bose stereo.
They call the police on the white cube truck parked
Over-night, every night in the parking lot in front of their
apartment.

Widow

With her folks in Oregon, we saw the word.
Later, after, we tended the courtyard,
with its potted rosemary,
transforming purple flowers into yellow and red.

We watched their cat Raymond Carver
make room. Later, when we visited
To make room. She had moved the books.

Oh and yes, there was a window in the kitchen
A low window in the kitchen with her
Flowers outside,
Their round red fists like hearts
Their round hearts like fists.

The courtyard, with its potted rosemary.
She had cherry tomatoes on her porch.

Outside the first ground floor apartment,
On the counter where the table pulled out,
the countries she never visited.

Near the candle shrine with its dried flowers,
She would take tea.

Later, when we visited to watch
Her heart grow back into nurturing,
We saw, the colorful yellow and red patterns
Of her new couch converted,
As it was, into a day bed.

Her hair grown back to brown.
Her cat called Raymond Carver,
Curled up into a basket.

From the inside wall, flowers spilling
Open onto the cracked concrete, into
in the concrete, open, as it was,
it was simple.
An apartment she rented after.
The apartments she rented later.

And basil, her new plantings of wild
Flowers and tomatoes
And basil, her new plantings of wild
transformations out of bleak.

In a Certain Village

The clothing all fit perfectly,
Especially a red cape made by
A specific woman for her
Less than specific daughter.

There was an unruly journey
And a patted cake with a minute
pot of yellow, whipped butter
peaceful as a softened heart.

There was a wild beast
of a tallish bad-mannered
man who said, "I'll go this way,
my dear and you go that."

There was a long illness,
Sort of like the flu or scarlet
Fever. There was a plain wooden
armoire and a grandmother.

This will end badly I think
we all know, don't we?
"Watch your back."
the girl's mother said.

Before the journey she
Cautioned, "the world is not
Always kind." This story is also
about a bed and a zippered knife

With a blood gauge. I warn you,
no one here is left to discuss
the legal terms, or the details of
what might have happened.

Later the village people will puzzle
About the incident, and they will
ask after the grandmother,
"Did she live far? And "Was it dark
when her journey began?"

Summer Vacations

Traveling cross-country
On the last full-service Amtrak complete
With a dining car,
Pullman porters and a view of "these" United States
Telephone pole, after telephone pole
I rode from California to New Bedford.

Losing Pepper doll's red flatzie
Eating corn flakes out of a box served by
A black man who whistled "Amabama" to himself,
I noted license plate letters on the cars below.

Another August, Hearst's Castle and the mistress
With my name, the blue indoor pool with gold electric tiles,
The Lancelot dining room with a million flags.

The machines at every Motel 6
From Los Angeles to Cottage Hills
That spit out cardboard
Cups of salty, perfect, parsley-topped chicken broth.

My Baby Tender Love, lost
In Luther Burbank's garden
Or the amazing underground caves of
Baldasare Forestiere in Fresno.

Throwing up in the parking lot
At Winchester Mystery House, then
Climbing the secret stairs where
Boxes of blue-green Tiffany glass
Stood inside an endless ballroom where no one danced,
But a ghost heiress.

The Space Needle paled
In comparison to the Woodsie Owl bumper sticker,
And the Japanese Pavilion with its folded paper
Swans and orange rice candy whose clear wrappers dissolved
In my mouth.

Victoria and Albert's museum dolls,
And Eva Xavier, my pen pal. Maui,
Where cousin Kimo, taught me to knee-surf,
Paddling off three sea-miles without dipping
My neck under water one July.

The Polynesian Cultural Center was the same
As the SS Arizona, but the coconut pancakes
And the virgin Chi Chi's
Are inked to my heart like a flower. Front Street with my dad,
In negotiation with the Portuguese men of his soul,
Over malasada.

My dad, who fried linguisa sandwiches in hot butter
And left us behind
Like shoes thrown over a street's power line stretched between
The two sides of our family.

For Lynda Hull

You smile at us, in folding
chairs. *Fiat Lux* and *Chiffon*.
The syllables curl into insignificant
worlds.

Turban-headed, hands gesturing,
you barely stay afloat at Duttons.

But this was before icy roads,
and missed stops.

Before shattered ankles and nights
awake. The crutches of friends.

How absolutely young we sat
while you searched the audience
for ex-lovers, joking like a bride.

For water, asking politely.
Between poems, between
the memory of a hospital bed,

a girlhood friend with AIDS,
drunk conversations in a walk -up
in China Town, a woman on a fire
escape—wearing nothing but
stockings,

stretching her back into the worlds
far away from the dark city of you.

Breaking with the Old

(italics loosely based on *Urban Dictionary* entry under New Bedford)

Breaking with the old, it was a grand adventure
to end all adventures. Leave Aunt Mary and Uncle John
and the city *on the south coast where you can eat linguisa
and Jag.* A place *where you know to stay away from
The Front after dark,* where you *head down to the Fort,
to light up or* make out, *knowing that the Guatemalans
all live in a van, you know that Sassaquin* Pizzao
*isn't really New Beige, but then you get dressed up
to go to the Madeira feast,* or the Holy Ghost.
And even you can prove the Dartmouth
*refs get paid off, you know that boys do play volleyball,
or they head to Puzzles if they're gay, market off to Strand if
underage, and troop to Bar 908 if they are forever*
resilient. *Our* Portuguese *fishing fleet is almost gone,
and everyone knows at least three people who deal.*
You leave back for *cruising on the Ave
until 2 on a Friday,* leave back where you are,
hitting up the 24 hour Dunky's, doing a turnaround at Brooks,
leave back where you are,
*and maybe laugh at the imports in the Wendy's parking lot,
laugh at the wall,* the great wall of New Bedford
Mass, I say *aka 20 aka the secret city aka the new war zone
Aka the new Bagdad aka the druggy capital* of the world,
Aka my drama city where the humidity
makes me throw up on Acushnet.
AKA the Standard Times. *Aka a violent city
aka a kaput city a dead city, this city wrapped around itself,*
in a zone of deadness inside a blind spot,
of lacking, where there is *a lot of underground talent,*
and no one wants to get caught in the after dark, tied down,
or led back to what they call "A New," or "the New,"
aka new beige. And here's the bit most people don't know
this but *it's called the secret city because there is no snitching
in New Bedford.* No one ever tells. New Beige, a place where half
of the hell of this city don't even speak.

If I Had Not Read the Book,
I'd Still Have Believed

Hanging there in white, a bride
of dried veil blossoms, alit
like an electrical
storm, a brutal spark or a stir spoon
of cream in gentle water but dry,
florescent, flushing, pale, solvent.
Solvent as a daughter vouchsafe, with
names like chamomile, hibiscus, hawthorn
devil's claw, lavender, night shade, honey
root, sarsaparilla, horseradish, myrrh.
My fingers are disappearing, now,
dissipating to powder. It was mortar and pestle,
a cold and fixed time in history.
Pagans. The Black Plague. Salem.
One sip of me could poison or
heal, tangoing down your backbone spine,
cold or dry or steaming, steeped
into a shade or overshadow of fresh tea,
brewed like a promise. Tea, drink in, stir
fast. This is not easy, lover, come to me
while whole. Come to me when I am
what is wanted, while effervescent, while
I am, white, while the mother stirs
on her axis, while there is a promise for-
While there is still—

Musings in January

I decided that it is not his body
although that perhaps
could have or used to have been
a reason and he is still pretty
but after watching a definitely B
chick flick in a hotel room
last weekend, it would suffice
to say that it is not, definitely not
the bull dog neck, which I also happen
to favor. Or the flat boxer's nose.
No, it is how in this hopeless movie,
and every previous film or still photograph,
or candid shot, he has made or posed for,
he looks at his women as if they
were a platter at a banquet, or ice
at an oasis, and he is an island surrounded
by water or a lake or he is a sailor.
And now he is lost, thirsty and lost.
So lost as if he wanted nothing more
than to drink in what all women in the universe
have to say
Even when he is starving, thirsty, dying,
Even then.
He would rather listen.

Arriving at the Place of the Pain

Arriving at the place
of the pain, there is street traffic,
and the moon is an ability
to float or fly above water or
the intensity of this why
and why not or how deliverance
from a year of crying happens.
It's been ten now and still
the human race is a different
location. The first death
of childhood, a neighbor
posed on her side ,under a sheet,
her body rolled down
the aisle of St Luke's on Termino.
On a weekday, she was Marion.
On the Saturday, she was white,
her life painted on in weekly sections,
the trim, the careful patches
under the eaves. The old paint
showing through. Her Pal Malls
in the cigarette case purse.
Her husband, boasting a stubbly beard,
his skin showing thru red blotches.
We found him sitting in the first row.
Arriving at the place
Of the pain, weeks later,
my mother and I surprised Mr Ed,
in his nakedness, pushing
the apartment door open we saw him
chasing a figure, a pink nightgown.
We'd been bringing by kale soup,
in a glass jar secured with a rubber band.
Arriving at the place
of the pain I hold it at arm's length,
away from sensation, into the deep.

Sundown Town

He gets in a mood.
He is a weed to pull out
Like in when someone's
Teeth weren't straight.
I seem so young ago.

Two houses are a long time
To wait. There is sun in the
Charleston garden and decorated
Chairs from Mary and Robert
From the auxiliary.

No one wants to die he said.
Life is painful enough
If it works, will the next
Past go away? Will the chest
Flutters soak into the skin
Like grey lime slurry. All lost things
Are not love, he said, unless
They are you and me between
Tomorrow. It's the right thing

To do. Whatever happened to the original
It was three past and counting.
A man in blue takes a seat
At my table without asking
And smiles in these decades
More than at any other time.
In a place where you are
The last person.

Start Here

It was like trusting
a stranger and letting
him into your house,
when you had a nagging
feeling he would turn
up later with a key.

Even as you answered
The door, saying
in an unfrightened
way, that you wanted
to be, were wanting
to be charitable,

There were thoughts
of a gang of men.
of him, just like this,
breaking
into your life,
throwing boxes,
looking for quick

answers, then
leaving behind
empty cartons.

Even when you tried
to put charity
first, you pictured
the unlocking
and a gun

You saw your
grandmother,
someone
asking for her
purse, then more.
Lots more.

Renovation

It's Sunday and he makes the mistake
of brandy. The flooring nearly done.

A terrible error, stepping back
to admire grout and rimed borders
like old battlefields he'd rather forget.

In no motion at all, he feels
the wall of malice, limbs freezing,
wires hanging from trees.

His wife, the work has ceased.
The solidity of existence pressing

against a metal fence prompts
the man to drop to his knees.
A changed man, returned to no fanfare.

As cars go by, triumphant against
the task at hand, he suffers. Across
the bathroom floor, he picks up his cutter

and begins again. Day after day, he crawls.
Every combat bone in his body, every
thing he can remember is a wall he cannot

shake. Hanoi. Ho Chi Mihn. The moon
in the open vault of heaven calls out to him.
A holy city inside his head. There is no material

he is familiar with, there. Pain
is not locatable. Not above his waist,
not where he can reach it.
Not even stones are this everlasting.

Arrhythmia

In the early days of the disease,
There is nothing else to call it,
We were giddy with guessing
Treatment, symptoms and hope.
We knew there was a pattern
and measures we could take.
Giddy and happy to have been
Saved again with a new rental
Agreement On life. There was
Recuperation that felt like healing.
The hope that things would get better.
There was a pathway stronger and clearer
To take. We mixed potions and meds
In a shoe box, each doctor visit an opportunity
To fine-tune the cocktail. You were young
For this sort of thing, a 40-something man
In a sea of waiting room seniors,
With much time to figure things out,
To get it right. A younger body heals
quickly, and each new year there are new
Drugs. Every time we blink there is a lab study,
Or a control group. There is time, more
Than time if you had gotten this at 70 or 80.
Still able to travel, enjoy life, even work
And drive. There was not a task or event
We mentioned except boxing that the doctor
Did not smile over and approve, explaining
That anything was possible. As if to tempt fate,
That first autumn, you got out of a sick bed
To build a new fence, jamming post piles
Into the ground with the same brute strength
You had at 20. Defying the odds. You used power
Tools and threw back bottles of the dark brandy,
You quit then started then finally quit. And then
Smoking the unfiltered Nat's you had favored
In college, dizzy with the promise of new life,
A new start. I was a new wife to you.
There were countries to explore, battles
to be fought, languages to adopt and twist
And make into our own.

The Well

for Jessica McClure

She focuses on a dark place,
a solid rock. A narrow dusk
somewhere with just enough
room for her below
the ground. Harder than granite.
She searches for a view
above the roar of bulbs
flashing, of spots,
of the color green.
This is her contest
with sleep, with pins
and needles, with the
boredom of waiting
for someone to help.
Trapped nearly two
days, a new plant's roots
the only arms holding
her back from hell. She struggles
to free herself—to stand up,
to leave. To just walk
away and laugh. Now.
There is digging above.
Jackhammers. A hole bored
large enough for someone to reach
in—but no one does. Yet not enough
room to crawl out. Pneumatic drills.
Only her nursery rhymes
penetrating the Texas air.
Sparks fly like stars
as large hands grow
closer, augers rumble promises.
She struggles to stand up,
but something holds her
back. Another song,
her mother's young

voice, still as October, inside
the house. She imagines
a man drowning
under dirt, her father taking
a photograph, then swinging her high
in his arms. Food.
Water. Her left leg bent
under her hip. Boring tools.
Without warning, one afternoon
her life became a wish. A game
of hide and seek with added
consequences. It was just a stone
she saw, perhaps, or a flower pot
covering a tunnel to eternity.
The voice said, Climb up, slide down.
It will do you good. She listened.

Like Nameless Skyscrapers

She carries him, still,
in her body. Embedded,
her lover soars somewhere
between pores and blood, rubbing
like broken glass. She owns
this enduring ache: his
inside hers, working,
working to take flight.

She has a cigarette and
as the rising smoke
hits the top
of the ceiling and disperses
into dust and light,
lingering on in the room,
she watches what remains.

More and more, these days,
while she stands still,
anchors fall from her hips,
grounding her far away
from his angels.

At night he is a cold bed
sheet she pulls over her
face to hide among so much clean
whiteness, soft wings to hold
fast, so much to be afraid of.

Now, in Indiana darkness,
she sits in a corn field ready
for harvest. Roots appear
at her elbows, descending downwards,
as she digs for lost stones in the earth.

While her breasts, entrapped
by feathered husks, swell full
of the wooden sap now running
inside her.

All around, branches reach,
and taunt her like nameless skyscrapers,
singing spirals, furrowing,
dropping seeds and petals and conversations
she never caught.

Words on the wing
tell her nothing, absolutely nothing.

Everything she wants to hear.

Swinging Open

for the youngest son

How impossible at that age
to lather up and take an open blade

to my cheek. To match father's
thumbs, cracking the rabbit's yielded

neck. Surrounded by lemon trees,
one quick motion, releases. stories

told around the picnic table.
No Ellis Island. Rifles meant for culling

lizards and desert prairie dogs. The pull
of the gun bringing fear I could reach.

Grandfather hid in a ship's barrel, accused
of murder in Petrepetzia. The unroofed patio

where uncle played mandolin
under plump summer evenings.

Adult faces shiny and red, full of warm
wine. The hutches waiting, covered.

Hot stew simmered in trust. Father's cough,
temporary. How I miss the night drives

to fig trees. Back home, father sits, pushing
carrots around on a paper plate.

My own core small, warm, and safe,
beating rapidly. How delicious

the world was when grandmother shook
the linen table cloth into the wind.

Together with me, Remember

Mother bought bachelor
buttons, over-blown as an injury,
mature, colorful, flowers.
I imagined them in a dream,
the purple descending
from the sky backwards
like beauty:
their round inflorescence,
self-effacing in blue, magenta,
yellow—and blanketing
my body of grief, their petals attached
to stalks without thread,
needles sewing nothing,
a green thread joined only
by a growing
choice, of hope to ascend,
towering over the ground,
and opening
at the tidewater these flowers
tight and compact in the moment
of their brightest joy. Cornflowers
falling from the sky like an afternoon
I had as a girl where everyone
was sheltered by blue hydrangeas,
and they all wished for love,
their brightest joy,
descending like
a careful iris, clutching yet
never diminishing before
the one single wretchedness
descending over the blossoms
my mother and I planted.

Under Different Conditions

They say once you have it
it does not go away, like a thirst
for liquor, a child, intelligence,
an abusive hand, a talent with
words, blindness, poverty,
a green thumb, perfect pitch.

They say it changes form,
hiding around corners of the
bloodstream, inside the bones
of imagination, in the minds
of worry, between the lines
of every poem you read.

They say it is not possible
to shake; some fight back
for years, others—a matter
of months; it is worse
than watching meals cooked
while being forbidden
to enter the kitchen, stomach
growling, tongue lolling out
of mouth, focused on the odor
of food. Salvation, dishes,
spoons always just out of reach.

They say it changes who
you are, how family treats
you, what strangers say. Words
to avoid, books not to read,
gifts like saplings are to be dodged
as well as playful animals.
Promises are assumed to be left
open-ended, like women who
never finish what they say,
letting the ends of words float

in the air, hoping, counting
on the fact that those around
them will sooner or later fill
in the mornings for them or—
"Write it; you can say this."
Breast Cancer. People might stop
and watch rooftops as an unexplained
plume of black smoke rises and changes direction above us.

The World in 2001

My Dad and me, we made fun of slackers
and weepers in Chelsea. People who didn't
make it to Columbia. Workers who lost
jobs. Girls who had babies out of wedlock.
Folks who couldn't save, didn't pay American

Express off at the end of the month or invested in bad
government bonds for the future. People who took out
equity loans and didn't pay off their first mortgage.

People who collected unemployment, didn't bathe
or shave, who ate fast food hamburgers and didn't
wipe their feet when entering a house. Fathers
who abandoned children, mothers on welfare. Homeless
who should just get it together and try harder. Drunks

and coke addicts who succumbed to temptation. Catholics
who went to church Sunday and treated others badly
the rest of the week. Boys who threw their lives away
on football and cigarettes. Teenagers who bought TransAms
and dropped out of life. Older people who stole butterscotch

from Ralph's and then lied about their age at Denny's.
We thought those who failed just didn't, those who failed
just didn't try hard enough and that anything could be
accomplished with a clean breath of ambition, care and love.

That New York and the Twin Towers would always
be there. All that, that it would be enough. We thought it mattered
when Audrey ate wheat germ and yogurt and did what
the doctor told her to do, the rounds of chemo and radiation,
that walking every day, walking every day to Bixby Park, would
make a damn difference, would ameliorate the unsmiling days
drawn
on the calendar we kept to the side of the fridge.

Amazing Grace

I'm shopping for Halloween candy
and back to school clothes with my dead

mother. She's telling me what to do. We
consider the price of a green coat with

a gray fake fur collar that fits me perfectly.
You already have too many

coats, she says, drifting off to the plastic
jack o' lanterns.
We both have to go

to the bathroom and the world
of the working seems instantly

thirsty. I report or try to report back
to the office, having taken

A two hour lunch. I think of the
impractical
nature of that coat I didn't buy.

It fit me perfectly, and I just knew it would
have lasted me her lifetime.

Whatever

And so I'll have to pretend
to be happy when the sheets
used for drapes begin to pull
at my heart. I'll have to be brave
and pretend to understand the
billowing "whys" no one can talk
about or explain without
long-winded journeys
of instructions or prodding
by a knife. I'll be the first
one to take charge like your
bride of the sea, then give
up and be lost where nothing
lives. It'll always be the same
way even when you're gone
and it's changed through
some other cycle of foul
weather, of similar
and comfortable oceans
with pitching boats.
Instead of wonderful and
distant, pull back like an island
and tie me off when you feel
needy as a rope. Try not
to last. Rub onions
on the gates of doubt.
Give in and don't tell
me the details. Push me
away when you feel
sad and the mileage
grows off course without
anyone left to think what
ever happened to those two
people marooned in California.
Magna Mater, from whom
the sun rises and into whose
arms it sinks. Whatever
became of love. Rage. Trouble.
War.

The Story of the Stories

The day before Easter is the last day of Holy Week, in which Christians prepare for Easter. This day commemorates the day Christ's body lay in the tomb.

Holy Saturday
Lasts until dusk

The altar un-covered
The church stripped

Of its riches.
Worshippers solemn

After the soul rises
Into the holy moment

Mojacar women gather
Pebbles from Rios Agua

Inside folded skirts
Padre Nuestra,

They recite
As they walk home

From the river
In their dark clothes

The store their prayers
And pebbles carefully

In a paper sack
Deep inside a drawer

Until winter
When from flat rooftops

The women throw
Resurrection pebbles

Into the first wind and rain
Of the cold season
To the left
To the right,

Thrown in the shape
of a cross.

The women chant
To make the storm retreat

They chant to make
An illusion. Like life.

Like Jesus himself
Arisen from the world.

Watering Day

Any water is fine; he travels
Between the two,
A bucket and a blue hose

Drenching cactus in its broad
Pots, and patches of rosemary.
From geraniums with their pink

And red blossoms, near houses close
So as not to lose out to the courtyard.
Water is scarce here in Mojacar,

To Sebastian, with his brown skin
And half-smoked cigarettes, watering
Just enough to ease the draught

For the tomatoes, the pimentos, the
Ancient almond trees inside the
Parameters of a sandy garden.

There are figs, more rosemary,
Most plants straggly with dust.
Planted alongside wilted lettuce,

In the nearly desert-like sun, the garden
Is slow and unimportant; there is just
Enough water to go around each season.

Sebastian's work, mostly focused
At the bottom of where the grove of almond
Trees starts, the trunks only a quarter kilometer

High. The housekeepers watch and mop
The adobe floor every eight or nine days.
Sweeping scorpions along with the dead flies.

And shutters, opening them roughly in the tiger
wind, showing their distain. The women have come
With their full buckets to clean.

Almonds

Troilus and Cressida: "The parrot will not do more for an almond'

As if someone has a conscience
From a long ago orchard,

Almond trees here,
Forgotten uneasily.

Ancient olive trees too, still
Bearing fruit, although

No one appreciates them.
The German girl gathers

A bowl of almonds and spends
An hour hammering them

Open. Some taste bitter
She says, I've wondered if

The bitter ones might be poison
Like the oleander.

Later, unsullied from a walk
She brings home flushed, wild

Grapes and brown carob
Pods found beside the road

To Mojacar Pueblo.
We eat slowly, understanding

A thing called Spanish pride
And a unity of purpose, wrapped
Together and tasting very much like hot, blind temptation.

Portuguese Bend

Every semester, Doc would take
His geology students from Long Beach City
to Mojave, the painted desert
Anza Borrego for unapproved field trips.
But his great delight was predicting
What would happen next at Portuguese
Bend, the last and largest area
of natural vegetation on the Peninsula.
Doc would look sideways at the road,
Following the black ribbon of ever-changing
reality, about how the tarmac had jumped
three feet since last semester.
The shaky red cliffs, that once held the future
Now left to wild, the opposite of development.
But that which was and is now unsuitable
for building also holds our planet's future.
He smiles in morbid glee, about his
Game of predicting the next house to
Fall. We crouched under stilts, walked gently
Across dried out lawns, examining the movement
Of the earth, the landslides, the slow slippage
Of time back into the sea. The Orange-crowned
Warblers, the coastal sage brush and the Pacific-Slope
Flycatcher our arms entangled with a species of
Love-forever Dudleya virens on the Peninsula headland.
Long before our field trips, this was the homeland of the
Tongva, for thousands of years before Portuguese explorer
João Cabrilho wrote of Chowigna and Suangna settlements
And of how Native Americans blessed Palos Verdes
I stoop to look under a house,
half fallen into the sea, leaning against itself
as if it were terminally ill. Soft. Weak.
Yellow caution tapes drawn around its waist.
Portuguese Bend, named after Captain Jose Machado
Who, sailing past Deadman's Island,
brought a crew of Azorean whalemen in 1864.

Taking barrels of oil from the blubber flenses
of gray whales off the coast of California.
The ground slips beneath my feet,
a slight landslide of broken rubble,
rock fragments, shale, sand and silt, basalt.
Hollow channels cut beneath the earth
form channels for soft zones to settle.

Mother Ditch

"We're trying to determine how best to keep it," Council District 1

I don't trust anyone
And love fewer than that.

Mother ditch was a water way
with an F sharp turn

A brief tongue below
The blue line
At the mouth of the LA soul.

Zanja Madre
1788.

Yes, say it. You want
to feel the tide of the words.
In my chest
I hear your water pounding
Zanja Madre

I know you do,
water, I know you do
want to love me.

Zanja Madre
Is where women
Washed clothing.

She welcomed all
who came to her.

All who let her run free
And, those who tamed
with red
Bricks like dark skirts
And Spanish words.
A soft whispered vow

of a rush to continue
on in this life.

Zanja Madre

She gave me her word
Los Angeles, she carried aqua,
To a blossoming pueblo.

Yes, I repent, yes I repent.
I let everyone down
By getting old and still

The water sped
Underground me like a brief harmony
Like a song belted out
When a child is near by

For always, we said.
Yes, for always.

Once there was a brick tunnel
Encasing her water body

And she was there making room
for Chinatown.

Mother ditch.
Zanja Madre
Precious water to the pueblo.

A life found. A life lost.

We are open, construct me.
We are hidden, take me apart.

Go to our hearts, Angelinos.
We are still here.

Mother ditch make mine
Me. Make ours always
Make ours this. Make me
Mine. Home Make us ours. Yes.

After She Got her Nose Fixed

She looked like Lena Horne.

But, it wasn't on a day to day basis,
Except for, in the light of a bar,
She was really something.

Then, she got seedier and seedier
In those old days, rents were cheap
And all the artists moved in next
Door to the bookies in Venice.

She knew the names of the
Tracks, the tricks, the men who
Paid up and those who didn't.
She knew which Laundromat
To read magazines in.

After she got her nose fixed,
We'd sit outside the Lincoln
Apartments, and watch
Our kids in Mother's Park.

Once, the nine month old
Climbed up the elephant slide
Right to the top and then jumped
Off. As if we were gonna spit, we laughed.

After she got her nose fixed,
She memorized the homeless
On Speedway and knew each sign
By heart like a television commercial:
"Will work for 4-20 hook-up."
"I won't lie, I want the money for beer."

When they were flush,
She suffered herself as a gift—To them, as if she was
    a new breed of love.

There Was a Part

Of something that made it OK
For you to smoke Marlboros first
In front of our parents, have a child
Barely into wedlock and cuss
At mom on the front lawn in Kentucky
While we watched mealy-mouthed,
All impressed, clutching Peachie notebooks.

There was a part of something,
Big Sis, that paved the way for me
To talk to boys on the phone, to sit
Quietly like a student while you drank
Beer with grandpa Joe and smacked
Your lips. There was a part of something
To be admired, your lack of guilt—all the promises

And the special pet things we got, you found
Allusive, struggling in your own black sheep
Kind of way out of the forest of mental
Illness our family brought you into.
There was a part of something, that made you
A trail blazer, the hero who landed on her feet
In the borderline middle of nowhere while I took
First Communion

There was a part of something that you were
The one to aspire to, to talk gossip about and,
Ultimately, I was not be brave enough to be.

There was s part of something that, even when
I'd settled down to my own Walmart lot in life,
You rose above. Out of touch, disappearing

Years ago, but I can still image your days, full
Of randomness. In an official helicopter,
you're a pilot full of border crossings and contraband,
Following a drummer around California,
or you are hired to guard a serial killer or the President.

I thought of you in prison or lost at sea, harboring
The map to where El Dorado is. When I close my eyes,
I can picture you rough, marked with daisy tattoos,
Staring down a postage stamp of LSD at a Motel 6,
Or looking through a telescope of Vicodin. I know you
Are holding a red badge of courage, a Nobel prize
And a purple heart, secretly in your breast pocket.

The Last Borges

Like God and his Eve,
you never passed on
your secrets; I struggled
to learn. Coitadinho, coitadinho.

Never sure which accent to
migrate towards; which window pane
to breathe on for the best cursive fog.
I shunned the loud
Portuguese fights.

The visiting relatives, named for saints,
over and over, in the driveway
at night, drunken Uncle John or Paul,
or Robert crashed his truck
into the side of our house:
filha da puta!

While you went to night school
two nights a week—for twenty years,
and ate linguiça sandwiches,
I watched and listened.

I would catch you: sitting at
Rudy the barber's chair
I would sneak up behind to hear
foreign words.

At school, I pronounced our name
as you taught me,
as an Englishman would:
flat and plain, riming it with
a word for "pretty."

After a while it seemed
that someone else

had heard a grandmother's
lullabies at night:
a verse that sounded like
a baby's cries for milk,
wanting the nipple:
Mamã eu quero, Mamã eu quero

As you grow older, papa,
I long for a language that joins us,
beyond our last name,
the space between our front teeth,
and wavy black hair.
Beyond linguiça,
kale soup and sweet bread.

But, the only Portuguese words
you ever gave me do not stand for love.
Que queres, que queres.
What do you want, what do you want.

Inventing the Present

from a line by Stephen Dunn

This time I stick through
the aches pulling at me

like the flu left alone.
To co-habitate, to move

back, these chains tightening.
Of coupling, the welcome

home into a comfortable time,
to a round object. The state

of two halves restored,
of being apple, then carved.

The feeling of wholeness
lost and returned.

The secure luxury of
being on the tree, fearless.

Back into ripe growth
and then magically fused

with another. That happens.
The lull, coming home to a warm

body, the checking in. The awful
noise that ends where one

begins and is later part of two,
the noise you hate but cannot vocalize.

Each time stopping to sing, apologizing
to the earth for the rest of your life.

Ordinary

Seemingly overnight her breasts grew
fat and the moles appeared. I don't know
why we never questioned it; we might have,
today, just how she moved from wife to
grandmother. How she was when he died.
How the dentures and the gray hair, the soft
gray hair, the thick gray hair appeared.
Her habits of stuffing tobacco into the furniture
drawers that none of us could believe even
after a lifetime. And she had all but answered
our questions, so alone in her counterfeit
elderliness, in exile. Heavily-ridged red polished
fingernails, the Evening in Paris perfume, the awful
rubber over-shoes. We never mentioned anything,
even after we had already called her ghost-name
in the root cellar for years, and I had sworn
that my grandfather was buried under the flowers.
The lilies powerful because of what remained
in the empty guest house. Far away from New York
in the 1920s. I used to think she missed her
daring job as a telephone operator on a street
I once heard my mother call out loud on a car trip.
I assumed that grandmother would know why I never
questioned this either. The new name I gave her,
Margo. After all, I was too young to understand. God
only knows—but Grandmother did and broke her
hip with an orange ball, balancing in the kitchen
with me like they did in the circus.

What the Water Gives Me

based on a painting by Frida Kahlo

At first it gives heat, burning red angels
on my ankles when the steam from the bath
rushes in. If I don't find something in him
to hate, soon, I will be hurt. Motion,

not heart, undertakes every marriage.
The same way long burning
cigarettes fracture jerry-built ashtrays,
my body now cracks. The way the heart

of a bread loaf amasses mold: red
around the rim, green in the center.
Jealousy, then pain. All I wanted
from him. Nothing he wanted to give.

Running scared, what looks like boredom
to him is how I heal myself: the nagging,
invisible gin, something I need, but cannot see,
something I see, but cannot need, stains

from tea bags left in porcelain overnight,
while I waited for his return. In the dark
once I danced all by myself. The outside
window view of a hooded palm tree

looks just like a fist with a gypsy
bracelet engraved, "Penelope, forever."
How he makes me feel when he lets me
rub his neck before bed. Everywhere,

now, the bath water brews a thin mattress
for me to rest upon. My toes kick at the
drowsy skyscrapers in the tub; my arms extend
out for what I see: the women in turbans,
the men with eggshell eyes, the children
with their soft, miscarried faces.

The Mass

The priest who devours
himself as sacrifice
invokes the Latin words
for
Take this
my body
Take this in memory of me.

Burn this house
He says, burn it
with the secret
fire of philosophy,
a fiery form of water.

Burn it with supplication,
honor among the willful,
his own brand of
vertical theology,.

Make life into sudden
Food,
Wine for a bloody immaculate
escape.

Burn this
He says taking
what
he can separate from each palm:

the right-hand pages, the references
to eternity, the Song
of Solomon, the great voices
of Jack in the Pulpit.

Reverence.
Burn this he says,

Letting his soul
savor pain
uncrowded by regret
or remorse. Burn this,
smaller and smaller
thing
like a piece of paper
like a soul
burning in
circles from the sun
Like nothing
I have ever seen before.

Entirely, he steps outside
his world,
Not knowing
what he has been given
is
a prayer.

If not this birth—
This earth
A burning,
this wonderment
without smiles—
then nothing at all.
Yes, nothing, he says.
He says. Nothing.

Honest Words

This is the sickness that people don't get
better from. The evening that doesn't
evaporate.

I watch his hips move. His chest, a sea
of straight pins, and, while I hold him,
the aroma of new wood.

Should taste his salty skin?
Or bury my head in the round ocean
that is his shoulder, pretending also
to be asleep? No, I am human.

A half body resists what a whole body
wants. Wait for it.

I fold my hands up into prayers, Novenas
spoken. I dream. How can I distance myself?
Out-run his caress like a old sea terrace?

He wakes and each question is a test,
a piece of driftwood. A reason not to.

Is he willing me far away? Or am I tracing
a slow circle back to him from the heat
of his back against mine?

Ah. I think, a quick pull of the lungs will do.
His moan is not what I expected. Not what I was
swimming away from.

The tricks have worked before
with the others but he has set me aside like a child
who has done wrong. No. Thank you. Stay right here.

Through the sheets I feel his sleep-rhythm, his rise and fall. Am I waiting for him? Or am I wanting, ever wanting, the soul that was once inside me.

Outside me now. Rushing in. If only for a crude conversation, a touch without.

Faith

At night the careful hands
of nuns tuck underneath poker-faced
hips, and braid spirals. Spurious
dry fingers comb, wrap around,
and memorize a lost art.

They rock quietly against the mattress
and dream of things
they will not do.

Outside the cloister
a milky statue of the Virgin Mary
stands. Arms

collected,
face cast down, shielded by
Botticelli's wreath; under half lids
stony, rambling, the eyes breathe.

The marble skirt encloses other eyes,
petals too. While faithful prayer-sitters
speculate humidity,

the pedestal's scalloped
edge embeds Mary's feet
in Venus's half-shell.

From inside the white-washed convent
the inhabitants rush to
genuflect in disinfectant and soap.

Too fluid
for focus, they stop, now
and then, to gaze through
the thick third floor
curtains at the statue below

where Sunday children touch
Mary's stone breasts and place
potted roses at her feet,
wishing, wishing.

As young girls, nuns nodded
God's halo around their hair
and lit single candles. When the mother
superior lifted their veils
she offered wax for sealing.

After the benediction,
like the newly
dead, nuns don
solemn white.

The only other color
they ever wear flows onto cotton
rags between
their thighs.

This stale aired extra room,
this end of a knot,
this jump into frozen water,
this daughter waiting for words,
every month,
it requires this cardinal leap of faith
for them to still
believe
they
are
female.

Special thanks to
Dr James Ragan, Evelyn Conlon,
Frank Gaspar, Gerald Locklin, Vamberto Freitas,
Richard Aloia, Michael Khandelwahl,
Catherine Goddard and April Coloretti.

Grateful friendship to
Karen Hatcher, Marty Brown, Leticia Hernández-Linares,
Manuel Paul Lopez, Juan Luis Guzmán, Laurie Ann Guerrero,
Luivette Resto, Robert Manaster, Celeste Guzmán Mendoza,
Gloria Amescua, Ire'ne Lara Silva, Eduardo Corral,
Donna Barnard, Carolina Ebeid: The FACA crew:
Amy Sayre Baptista, PaulA Neves, Luis Gonçalves,
Carlo Matos; the Westside Women Writers: Kathi Stafford,
Lois P. Jones, Maja Trochimczyk, Sonya Sabanac,
Georgia Jones-Davis, Madeleine Butcher, Susan Rogers.

MILLICENT BORGES ACCARDI is the author of four poetry books: *Injuring Eternity*, *Woman on a Shaky Bridge*, *Practical Love Poems* and *Only More So* (Salmon, 2016). The recipient of fellowships from the National Endowment for the Arts (NEA), Fulbright, CantoMundo, Creative Capacity, the California Arts Council, Fundação Luso-Americana, and the Barbara Deming Foundation (Money for Women), Accardi has been in residence at Yaddo, Milkwood in Cesky Krumlov, Fundación Valparaíso in Spain; Jentel, and Vermont Studio Center. She holds degrees in English literature and writing from California State University, Long Beach (CSULB) and the University of Southern California (USC).